*Quick*GUIDES
everything you need to know...fast

PUBLIC RELATIONS

by Wendy Scaife

reviewed by Kathy Young

WIREMILL
PUBLISHING LTD

Across the world the organizations and institutions that fundraise to finance their work are referred to in many different ways. They are charities, non-profits or not-for-profit organizations, non-governmental organizations (NGOs), voluntary organizations, academic institutions, agencies, etc. For ease of reading, we have used the term Nonprofit Organization, Organization or NPO as an umbrella term throughout the *Quick* Guide series. We have also used the spellings and punctuation used by the author.

Published by
Wiremill Publishing Ltd.
Edenbridge, Kent TN8 5PS, UK
info@wiremillpublishing.com
www.wiremillpublishing.com
www.quickguidesonline.com

British Library Cataloguing in Publication Data
A catalogue record for this book is available from the British Library.

ISBN Number 1-905053-19-3

Printed by Rhythm Consolidated Berhad, Malaysia
Cover Design by Jennie de Lima and Edward Way
Design by Colin Woodman Design

Disclaimer of Liability
The author, reviewer and publisher shall have neither liability nor responsibility to any person or entity with respect to any loss or damage caused or alleged to be caused directly or indirectly by the information contained in this book. While the book is as accurate as possible, there may be errors, omissions or inaccuracies.

CONTENTS

PUBLIC RELATIONS

Introduction

What Is "Public Relations"?

What PR Can Achieve

What's Special About Nonprofit PR?

PR Professionals

Using Consultants

Research

The PR Plan

Planning

Implementing the Plan

PR on a Shoestring

Evaluating Performance

Final Thoughts

Introduction

" **P**ublic Relations (PR)" is as its name implies – it is about relating to and having a relationship with the public. The assumption, of course, is that the relationship is a good one. However, PR as a profession has received much negative publicity when it has been used to influence or limit the exposure of bad decisions by companies and organizations. As with any relationship, there must be a commitment to honesty and open communication, and to remain healthy, it requires a lot of work.

Far from being a means to manipulate an audience, PR is founded on ethical and honest communication. Hence, if the reality in an organization does *not* match the image being projected, public relations professionals are responsible for highlighting this to colleagues.

PR is a recognized profession, with a body of knowledge and a recognized skill set that can benefit the commercial and nonprofit sectors in many ways. It has a broad role that is taught at universities, often as part of a business degree.

PR is all about communication. But more precisely, it is about *managing and planning* communication between your organization and the many people and entities important to its survival and growth.

INTRODUCTION

It is incumbent upon PR practitioners to make themselves aware of relevant laws and best-practice considerations in the country where they operate. Many countries will have codes and laws such as a donors' bill of rights, guidelines on privacy, codes of conduct in e-marketing and the like. Public relations staff belonging to a professional institute will also be bound by its code of practice and ethics.

This book defines PR and some associated terms, illustrates what PR can achieve, and shows how to research, plan and implement an effective PR strategy for a nonprofit organization (NPO). It is an invaluable resource for experienced and novice PR practitioners alike.

Public relations touches all aspects of communication both within and outside your organization. The aim of PR is to optimize communication between your organization and the many people and entities that influence its existence.

Reviewer's Comment

The ideal is that 99 percent of your communication is planned, well presented and properly placed. A robust PR professional and well-organized organization can cope with the 1 percent of impromptu, emergency or responsive communication that may be required due to an unplanned event or crisis.

PR is also about *two-way* communication. Public relations professionals provide information about their cause, but they also solicit data and opinions from stakeholders.

PR is related to, but not the same as, marketing, advertising, publicity, promotion and integrated marketing communication. Definitions abound and vary for each of these terms.

Commonly, the following distinctions might apply.

- ■ "Marketing" is the art of making someone desire something that you have. It involves an exchange between a consumer and an organization, and may involve advertising of core products and services or a less direct promotion of the organization and its image and values.

- ■ "Promotion" is a general term for various communication tactics such as advertising, selling, offering bonus with product, and publicity.

What Is "Public Relations"?

- "Integrated marketing communication" or IMC is a term coined to describe a unified communication effort. It blends various communication techniques and tools (such as advertising, marketing, promotion, public relations, research, strategy, and evaluation) to achieve a unified and consistent set of messages from an organization.

- "Advertising" is your message, as you want it said, which you pay various media to feature.

- "Publicity" is free coverage in different media of an event, launch or discovery which has usually been initiated by the organization.

These different types of communication are *tools* within the public relations kit. Professionals will often specialize in one of these fields. So a nonprofit PR person may outsource work to an advertising agency, market research firm, special-events consultancy or all of these. Overlap among the different disciplines is common. Sometimes in-house practitioners may bring all of these skills to their cause, depending on their background, training and experience.

What is the relationship among fundraising, development and public relations?

- Generally, PR creates the climate in which fundraising and development occur.

- Development is the process of identifying, cultivating and building relationships with potential supporters and then maintaining a strong stewardship program after the gift, which keeps them informed and acknowledged so their support is a fulfilling experience that is likely to be ongoing.

- Fundraising is the actual asking.

WHAT PR CAN ACHIEVE

An effective PR person or team can offer many benefits to NPOs.

Some PR activities may have an impact on the work undertaken by the organization. For example, PR can:

- Make the organization's views on particular issues known.

- Involve opinion leaders in the work of the organization.

- Identify potentially controversial issues that are relevant to the organization's work.

- Change people's behaviour with regard to a particular issue (e.g., encourage people to stop smoking, to get regular health checks, to recycle plastic, etc.).

- Achieve legislative change in the interests of beneficiaries, by bringing pressure to bear on local or national governments.

- Engender positive feelings toward the organization among those with the power or influence to help the NPO meet its goals.

PR can also help the organization with its own public profile. For example, PR can:

- Increase the level of public awareness of the organization generally.

- Generate accurate perceptions of the aims/work of the organization.

- Minimize the impact of negative publicity.

- Reposition a cause or an organization that may have become tired or the subject of misconceptions.

- Raise awareness of fundraising opportunities, in order to increase income.

Crucially, it is important to identify the needs of the organization that PR is intended to satisfy.

WHAT'S SPECIAL ABOUT NONPROFIT PR?

A cause can be looked at like a product, but sometimes this approach is too narrow and commercial to work in a nonprofit setting. Many nonprofits do aim to change the world or at least the world of those who benefit from their work. They are about highlighting society's issues and engaging people in their mission, not just "selling" a "cause."

PR in a nonprofit organization needs to adapt (versus adopt) the best of commercial public relations thought to fit a nonprofit culture. Even in very large organizations that may have a staff of public relations professionals, the terrain differs from for-profit communication work.

Differences include:

■ Volunteers

■ Budget

■ Resources

■ Salaries

■ Level of emotional attachment to the job

■ Competition dynamics

■ Messages

■ The relationship between the organization and those it desires to reach

The work of a PR team is wide-ranging and varied, and depends on the structure of the organization. It is likely to involve any or all of the following tasks:

- Responding to queries from the media.

- Proactively placing information at the media's disposal.

- Cultivating relationships with particular journalists or media partners.

- Researching those audiences which are key to the organization's success.

- Researching the means of reaching those key audiences.

- Researching the views of members of the public on relevant issues.

- Planning strategies for one-off campaigns or as part of an ongoing plan.

- Selecting suitable channels of communication to achieve agreed upon aims.

- Establishing and comparing standards regarding communication strategies with peer organizations.

- Researching and disseminating information about upcoming events and publicity opportunities.

- Making sure that a photographer is present at all functions and events so that promotional materials are enhanced. (Secure rights and permission to use photographs when taking pictures of clients and staff.)

- Acquiring celebrity support and managing that/those relationship(s).

- Managing internal communications and employee relations (e.g., through newsletters or information programs).

- Establishing and maintaining a website for the organization.

- Looking after the NPO's image or brand and ensuring that it projects a consistent image at all points and in all print materials including business cards, letterheads, envelopes, posters, tickets, newsletters, magazines and advertising copy.

- Leading or managing an organization's marketing strategy.

- Developing relationships with key people in government or fields relevant to the cause.

- Developing relationships with people at key referral points (e.g., health workers, lawyers, financial advisors, estate planners).

- Managing the external messages from the organization (e.g., preserving the dignity of beneficiaries may mean not portraying them as "victims" or "sufferers").

- Managing community relations (e.g., public participation, community consultation and corporate community partnerships).

- Organizing special events, such as launch parties, conferences, photo shoots.

PR work may be performed in a nonprofit by personnel of various experience levels, by volunteers and/or staff, sometimes in-house and sometimes with consultancy input.

Different causes and types of organizations may need different skills. In reality, many nonprofits will have tight budgets that determine the skills they can "buy" either by hiring staff or outside consultants.

PR practitioners will develop their own skills as they gain wider experience while doing the job. So a very new practitioner may not be the ideal person to run a campaign of influencing the government, but he or she might be well suited to creating awareness through the media. Sometimes additional skills can be accessed through recruiting a board member or committee volunteer, or by outsourcing projects.

Using Consultants

One way to operate cost-effectively is to harness expertise on a voluntary basis. Often consultancies may work "pro bono" for an NPO, donating the time, creative work and expertise that your organization lacks.

If the relationship with such volunteers is well managed and the experience proves a positive and rewarding one, these professional volunteers may continue to work with your organization for a long time.

It is vital to treat volunteers appropriately. To make pro bono and volunteer relationships work, provide written briefs for the work they will undertake, allow them real involvement in your mission, offer appropriate supervision by and connection with paid staff, and give recognition of their work.

Be aware, however, that work for an NPO on a voluntary basis will generally have less priority than work for a paying client. Many times this won't matter, particularly if the work is not time-sensitive.

Sometimes, however, paying an experienced consultant or freelance PR person for a fixed period may be the most appropriate option, particularly if the work is required under time pressure or if the work is highly specialized.

If you do seek to hire a consultant or freelance person, ensure you provide him/her with a specific brief of the work to be undertaken and ensure both parties understand what work is required, when it will be delivered and the cost for such activities.

KNOW YOUR NONPROFIT'S "PUBLICS"

A "public" is a defined and reachable segment of people and entities that an organization has a ready affinity with and seeks to communicate with.

Typical "publics" of a nonprofit include:

- Clients or consumers (e.g., patients, if a health organization)
- Family and friends of clients and consumers
- Volunteers
- Donors (individuals and families)
- Staff
- Governments (all levels, elected and bureaucratic members, individual relevant departments)
- Trusts and foundations
- Service clubs
- Companies (small and large, private and public)
- Industry/professional associations
- Related organizations
- Schools/educational institutions (or other youth-market bodies)
- Financiers (banking/investment advisors)
- Supporter referral points (e.g., financial advisors, lawyers, accountants, estate planners, fundraisers, consultants)

Reviewer's Comment

Depending on the organization's cause, the main task is to identify who may influence your organization positively or negatively and to plan some sustained and meaningful communication with them.

Working with opinion leaders from these "publics" can be a cost-effective way of making an impact where it counts, even with a minimal PR budget.

DEFINING YOUR EXTERNAL ENVIRONMENT

PR should involve research into the external environment in which the organization operates. This can be done formally through market research or informally through talking to people or surfing the Net. Research should include:

Continues on next page

- Which are the organization's publics?

- Who are the key points of contact (both within your organization and a specific public)?

- What is the public perception of your organization, of the issues you deal with, and of other organizations that work in the same field?

- What do these people do, think, buy, read, or watch? The more you know about them, the easier it is to target communications appropriately.

- What channels of communication are available to reach these publics?

- With what or whom does your organization compete to reach these publics?

Influencing people's behaviour can be a long-term commitment, requiring social marketing skills and an in-depth understanding of human behaviour. Research is vital to understand people's feelings on a subject, and to know how different publics are likely to respond to different messages or react to the different ways in which a message might be presented.

Reviewer's Comment
Ultimately, you must be prepared to communicate with everyone. You need to make sure you can tell the story of your organization in a concise and meaningful way to someone who knows nothing about it. Defining your support base is about building allies, who help you by way of their own participation and expressions of loyalty.

THE PR PLAN

If PR is about planned, two-way communication, what are we really talking about? A typical plan will address and quantify how an organization achieves its strategic, long-term objectives through the daily, weekly and monthly implementation of activities that inform and encourage support from a variety of "publics."

A PR plan should be reviewed and amended annually so that everyone knows what communication strategies are being used when, why and to what effect. And to be really effective, you also need to have a plan for your next crisis.

Reviewer's Comment
Good planning ensures that when the inevitable crisis does happen (and it will), the organization can immediately go into damage control instead of panic response. Also remember, a crisis is something that happens outside the plan – and it can be a really good thing which happens unexpectedly that you wish to maximize to your publics. The crisis management plan will dovetail with your PR plan in terms of accountability and systems.

When done over an annual calendar, you will be able to see whether there are gaps of time when your organization is not "talking," and you will also see potential conflicts (e.g., the road race occurring two days AFTER the mailing of your newsletter). It is important that all parts of your organization contribute to the annual plan so that all information about the organization can be communicated to its publics appropriately.

Probably the most important task in the planning process is to determine the key publics, identify their opinion leaders, and define how your organization will manage its communication with them to achieve its mission. Like all plans, it will work best when it is well defined with measurable objectives that lend themselves to straightforward evaluation.

A nonprofit public relations plan depends very much on the size and scale of the task and the nature of the organization. The RACE formula is much used in the formulation of a plan. It stands for:

- **R**esearch
- Plan the **A**ction
- **C**ommunicate
- **E**valuate

It emphasizes that public relations is a process – not an event.

As a general guideline, a PR plan should include the following:

- Summary of current situation – the result of research.
- Goals and objectives (these should be specific, timed and measurable).
- Key target audiences/publics/markets.
- Strategies (e.g., targeting print media that are read by people in the 17–25 age group, to try to engage them in the work as the supporter base ages).

- Tactics/action plan/timetable (the actual means of communication, such as newsletters, speaking opportunities, press releases, brochures).
- Evaluation tools and strategies.

Fundamental elements of the plan should include:

- Periodic newsletter – printed and electronic.
- Sustained flow of press releases, minimum of once per month.
- Scheduled special events, functions, launches.
- Scheduled advertising as appropriate.
- Updated and interactive website and links to it.
- Intentional and consistent internal communication strategies.

What communication strategies and tools work best?

Only through trial and error and measuring the results will you really find this out. However, popular means of communicating with key audiences include:

■ Publications such as newsletters, magazines, reports – either in print or electronic form – sent out directly from the organization to supporters, beneficiaries, partners or other publics.

■ Direct contact (e.g., public speaking to groups, conferences, functions).

■ A website that offers information, bulletin boards, a library and current calendar of events. Increasingly websites provide the opportunity for people to donate to as well as express interest in the organization. All communication should drive your publics to your website for more information.

■ Media publicity including press releases and other information sent to newspapers and magazines (international, national, regional, local, special interest, trade, and consumer), TV and radio.

■ Paying for advertising or advertorials (advertorials are advertisements that appear as articles).

■ Eye-catching events, one-off promotions, special events (e.g., Organization Week, launch events, opening ceremonies, thank-you receptions, celebrity visits).

■ Community events – library buses, walk-in centres, poster campaigns.

Whatever means you use, remember one golden rule:

Journalists and editors care primarily about filling their pages or time slots with stories that are newsworthy and that will interest their audiences.

Continues on next page

It isn't their job to promote your organization – it is yours! They will not help you simply because you have a good cause, but they will cover your story if it is newsworthy and of interest to their readers (or viewers or listeners).

Know as much as you can about the medium being asked to promote your organization or to cover its activity or to run its story. An essentially visual story won't fit a radio program nor will a current affairs program be best for airing a sports story.

Therefore, your communications need to grab the media's attention, have an interesting angle, offer something novel or quirky, and target the same audiences that each particular media outlet is trying to reach.

The limited resources and minimal budgets of most NPOs call for creativity, commitment and innovation to maximize PR impact. Here are some ideas:

- Recruit and make use of volunteers, providing you have the capacity to manage them well.

- Use leverage (e.g., pay for advertising space and negotiate three or four times that amount in coverage to be donated by media outlets).

- As part of a partnership with corporate supporters, negotiate access to their public relations expertise, consultancies and media buying power.

- To avoid doing the same work many times, draft an "internal case statement" – a large document that covers everything anyone wants to know about your organization and cause. From this "information bank," you and others can draw out most facts, figures and phrases you will need for the many communication pieces you will create. This also creates a layering of similar images and messages that build up a consistent picture of your cause in the minds of your key publics.

Reviewer's Comment
This is also your readily accessible "background" information when you find yourself in a crisis.

- Make use of community service/ public service announcements to avoid advertising costs.

- Have the organization's car branded so people see the NPO "in action" around town.

- Provide business supporters with framed appreciation certificates for their office lobbies.

- If your key business partner sponsors an annual event, ask if you can obtain additional publicity by presenting an award or certificate at the function.

- Locate a media partner who will promote your cause for free or for a discounted rate.

Continues on next page

- Piggyback communications to key publics by including your material with mailings that are already going out from corporate supporters to their customers and clients.

- Carefully tailor and target communication to those publics that your research suggests will be most likely to support you.

- Maintain your database carefully – eliminate duplicates and update it promptly when told of a supporter who has passed away or moved out of the area.

- Use email effectively and preferentially to make quick and continual contact in addition to saving on postage and printing costs.

- Collaborate with peers through professional bodies or peer mentoring to avoid costly mistakes and generate savings. For example, check for campaign clashes, forge appeal partnerships, jointly purchase media space, or loan (with due approvals) expertise and images. Find out what related causes are doing regionally and internationally, and suggest combining forces or sharing information and resources.

Following are some real-life examples of NPOs using creativity to get results, with minimal resources:-

- A small organization with low visibility gained significant coverage by creating a "Communicator of the Year" award for a local business leader/media celebrity.

- A medical research group built strong media relations (and thus secured an outlet for current and future stories) by running a "Scientist for Two Days Program," in which white-coated journalists were invited into its laboratory to follow each stage of an experiment hands-on.

- A small organization positioned itself as a national leader in its field by securing the placement of its CEO at business conferences and establishing him/her as an authority on nonprofit issues.

EVALUATING PERFORMANCE

Measuring and reporting successful outcomes (not just activities) against key performance indicators is one way to convince the boards and staff of NPOs to invest in and reward public relations activities.

There are different ways to measure success. The crucial consideration is whether the method chosen adequately and appropriately provides information to you and your organization about the results of the PR activities.

Some evaluation is objective and can be measured in numerical or cost terms. The more difficult evaluation is subjective, where thoughts and perceptions are changed by the activities.

Some objective questions that can be asked are:

- How many inches of column space did a press release generate? What would the same amount of space have cost in advertising? (The same evaluation can be done by understanding the cost of radio and television advertising and approximating the length of coverage the organization received in those media formats.)

- How many people had the opportunity to see, hear or read about a particular story as the result of PR activity? What was the exposure level through all media?

- How many people responded to a fundraising event as a result of media coverage – radio, TV or newspaper?

- How many times is your website visited?

Continues on next page

■ What is the circulation of your newsletter? How many people have asked to receive it? If you have a response mechanism, did you learn what percentage of readers used it?

A more expensive option is to pay for consumer research, which answers the following questions:

■ How many times has the organization's name been quoted correctly in the media in the last year?

■ What percentage of the public is spontaneously aware of your organization?

■ What percentage of the public recognizes the organization's name when prompted?

Measuring the impact of PR work in these ways is often done by agencies. To evaluate progress, it needs to be done both before and after a PR campaign.

The evaluation by subjective means can involve determining:

■ What the public perception of the organization is before and after the PR campaign.

■ Whether the public understanding of the organization's mission is accurate.

Evaluation of thoughts and perceptions may be done by survey, focus groups or other methods and, as noted, often is done by specialist agencies.

FINAL THOUGHTS

The role of public relations for NPOs is wide-ranging and valuable. The communication that an organization has with its publics defines what it is, how it is perceived, and determines ultimately how successful it will be. All too often PR is something that organizations hope to achieve almost by chance.

Establishing a planned and systematic approach to PR and managing it carefully can bring significant benefits. There are many opportunities for creative PR practitioners to achieve a positive community profile without high expenditure. This is the challenge of PR in the nonprofit sector.

WENDY SCAIFE

Wendy Scaife, BbusComn, MbusMgnt, PhD, FPRIA, MFIA, is a Senior Research Fellow at the Queensland University of Technology's Centre of Philanthropy and Nonprofit Studies (CPNS) in Brisbane, Queensland, Australia, where she researches and lectures in nonprofit management, fundraising and marketing. She is a Fellow of the Public Relations Institute of Australia.

Her working life has included roles as an in-house public relations manager (setting up the organization's first public relations department); a consultant; a freelance writer; and the public relations/media manager for a growing nonprofit, the Leukaemia Foundation. Wendy became its CEO, leading a team of 100 staff members, and went on to help take the organization national and serve as its national Deputy CEO.

She has won awards for fundraising and public relations campaigns and for lecturing, and was a finalist in the Business Woman of the Year Awards. Wendy is involved in the research team on Australia's national project (Giving Australia) to uncover why, how and how much Australians give. Wendy is married with two children and chases cows on the family farm in her spare moments.

Kathy Young, Reviewer

Kathy Young has been in the fundraising/public relations industry for 18 years at a variety of charities in Montana and California in the United States, where she grew up, and in New Zealand, where she now lives. After receiving a Journalism Degree from the University of Montana in Missoula, she went to work for the YMCA.

Working for both a member of a larger organization and the central office of the same organization gave Kathy the opportunity to see and develop different communication strategies within the same national organization. The YMCA offered a professional development program, and a career highlight during those nine years as Marketing Coordinator, Communications Director and then Senior Program Director was coordinating a yearlong 125th anniversary celebration.

Nearly nine years in New Zealand have given Kathy a different range of experiences in fundraising and public relations at two charities, including the local branch of the New Zealand Red Cross. Currently with the University of Otago in Dunedin, Kathy serves as the Partner Relations Manager for the Advancement Campaign called "Leading Thinkers." She also does book reviews for the local newspaper and writes poetry when not out walking the dog.